THE WEALTH BLUEPRINT

UNLOCKING FINANCIAL FREEDOM

Master the Mindset, Strategies, and Impact of True Wealth Beyond Money

GEORGE H. BUHR

Copyright @ 2024 by GEORGE H BUHR. All right reserved

No part of this book, including the text or other material, may be reproduced or transmitted in any form or by any means, including photocopying, recording or other electronic or mechanical means, without the prior written permission of the copyright owner.

The information provided in this book is intended for personal use and educational purposes only, While every effort has been made to ensure the accuracy and completeness of the content.

DEDICATION

To everyone who dares to dream, takes bold steps toward financial freedom, and believes in the power of giving back. May this book inspire you to create a life of purpose, prosperity, and impact—for yourself and for the world around you.

ACKNOWLEDGEMENT

I would like to extend my deepest gratitude to everyone who has supported and inspired me throughout this journey. To my family and friends, thank you for your unwavering encouragement and belief in me. Your love and support have been a constant source of strength.

To the mentors, financial experts, and thought leaders whose work has shaped my understanding of wealth and success, I am truly grateful. Your knowledge and insights have been invaluable in crafting this book.

Finally, to you, the reader—thank you for taking the time to explore these ideas and for trusting me to guide you on your path to financial empowerment. May the principles within these pages help you unlock your full potential and build the life of wealth and impact you deserve.

TABLE OF CONTENTS

DEDICATION..................................2
ACKNOWLEDGEMENT......................3
PROLOGUE....................................6
CHAPTER 1: THE FOUNDATIONS OF WEALTH.......................................9
•Mastering the Wealth Mindset...........9
CHAPTER 2: FINANCIAL FREEDOM...17
•Financial Literacy...........................17
CHAPTER 3: BUILDING WEALTH THROUGH INCOME..........................26
•Creating Multiple Streams of Revenue.....................................26
CHAPTER 4: The POWER OF INVESTMENTS................................35
•Making Your Money Work for You.....35
CHAPTER 5: STRATEGIC SAVING......45
•Protecting and Growing Your Wealth.....................................45
CHAPTER 6: WEALTH CREATION THROUGH ENTREPRENEURSHIP.....55
•Leveraging Business Opportunities....55

CHAPTER 7: THE IMPORTANCE OF WEALTH PROTECTION……………………66
- Risk Management & Estate Planning……………………………………..66

CHAPTER 8: GIVING BACK…………………77
- Wealth Beyond Money and the Legacy…………………………………………77

EPILOGUE……………………………………86

PROLOGUE

In the pursuit of wealth, there are no shortcuts or magic formulas. It's not about instant riches or get-rich-quick schemes. True wealth—lasting, meaningful, and transformative—comes from a deep understanding of how money works, the mindset that drives financial success, and the disciplined strategies that allow us to build and protect what we've earned.

This book is not just another guide on how to make money. It's about redefining what wealth means in your life and giving you the tools to create a future of financial freedom, security, and legacy.

As you turn these pages, you'll discover that wealth is not confined to bank balances or material possessions. It's a mindset, a series of habits, and a journey that unfolds over time. Whether you're just starting out or looking to elevate your financial life, the principles shared here are designed to help you gain control, think strategically, and navigate the complexities of money in the modern world.

But even more than that, this book is about the power of transformation—the ability to reshape your relationship with money, and in doing so, reshape your life.

From understanding the foundation of wealth-building to mastering the art of investment, from protecting your hard-earned resources to exploring the lasting impact of giving back, the path to wealth is one of both personal growth and financial savvy. It's about learning to think like the wealthy, act with purpose, and build a life that goes beyond just financial success.

By the time you reach the last page, you'll not only have the knowledge you need to grow your wealth—you'll be ready to take bold steps toward a future where money works for you, not the other way around. Your journey to lasting financial freedom begins here, and it starts with the decisions you make today. Are you ready to take the first step?

CHAPTER 1: THE FOUNDATIONS OF WEALTH

Mastering the Wealth Mindset.

Wealth is not merely about accumulating money or assets; it's about how we think and approach the world around us.

Every financial success story begins with the same core element: mindset. If your thoughts are rooted in limitation, scarcity, or fear, your reality will reflect those limitations. But if you cultivate a mindset of abundance, possibility, and empowerment, you open doors to a world where wealth isn't just a dream but a natural consequence of the actions you take.

The idea of mastering the wealth mindset is rooted in the belief that the mind is the most powerful tool at your disposal. Just as an artist needs a canvas to create, or a scientist needs data to experiment, a wealthy person needs the right mental framework to build their fortune. This mindset is not something you're born with, but something you can develop over time, with intentional effort and practice. It's a shift from thinking about wealth as an external, unattainable force to understanding it as something that starts within, growing through daily habits, decisions, and beliefs.

Many people struggle with the concept of wealth simply because they don't believe they deserve it, or they've internalized the notion that financial freedom is only for the lucky or the well-connected.
But wealth, in its truest form, is not about chance. It's about recognizing the opportunities in front of you and being willing to step into them with confidence. This shift in perception is crucial. You can be a product of your environment, your upbringing, and the circumstances around you, but only if you allow them to define you. Or you can decide to

break free from these constraints and carve your own path.

To master the wealth mindset, the first step is to remove the barriers in your thinking. These barriers are often disguised as limiting beliefs—thoughts that tell you that you're not good enough, not smart enough, or that you can't succeed. These beliefs come from many places: childhood, societal expectations, past failures, and even the media.
 But the truth is, wealth is not reserved for a select few; it's available to anyone who is willing to think differently and take consistent action toward their goals.

A key element of a wealth mindset is the willingness to take responsibility for your own financial situation.
 Too often, people blame their circumstances or external factors for their lack of success. It's easy to say that the economy is tough, that opportunities are limited, or that wealth is out

of reach. But when you take full responsibility, you empower yourself to make the changes that will alter your financial future. The minute you stop blaming external circumstances is the minute you begin to see solutions instead of obstacles.

Equally important is understanding the difference between earning money and building wealth. Many people confuse these two concepts. Earning money is something that most people do—they work a job, exchange time for dollars, or run a business to generate income. But building wealth is something different. It's about creating assets that grow in value, allowing you to create passive income and achieve financial freedom.

Wealth is about making money work for you, rather than working for money. This shift in thinking can be profound, and it is a defining characteristic of those who truly master the wealth mindset.

A wealthy mindset also involves an openness to learning and growth. Those who are truly wealthy are never satisfied with the status quo. They are constantly seeking knowledge whether it's through books, mentorship, seminars, or new experiences that can help them improve their financial situation. The more you learn, the more you realize how much there is to know, and the more equipped you become to make smarter, wealth-building decisions.

Whether it's understanding new investment strategies, learning about personal finance, or simply gaining insight into how wealthy individuals think, continuous learning keeps you on the path to success.

An essential part of mastering the wealth mindset is the ability to overcome fear and embrace calculated risks. Fear of failure is one of the biggest obstacles to wealth creation. But the reality is, failure is part of the journey. In fact, many successful people have failed numerous times before they found their formula for success. The key is not to let fear stop you from taking action, but rather to learn from your failures and use them as stepping stones toward success. Every failure is an opportunity to learn, adapt, and improve.

You also need to cultivate patience. Wealth doesn't typically come overnight. The process of building sustainable, long-term wealth requires discipline, perseverance, and time. It's about making smart decisions consistently over the long run, understanding that instant gratification can often lead to short-term gains but long-term losses. Patience allows you to stay focused on your ultimate goals, even when immediate results seem elusive.

A wealth mindset isn't just about accumulating more for yourself; it's about abundance, generosity, and the desire to create positive change. When you cultivate the belief that there's more than enough for everyone, it opens up your mind to opportunities not just for yourself, but for others as well. Wealthy individuals understand the importance of giving—whether it's through charity, investing in others, or sharing their knowledge and resources. The more you give, the more you receive, not just financially but in terms of personal fulfillment, satisfaction, and the sense of impact you can create in the world.

This mindset can be applied in every area of life, not just finances. Whether you're building a business, investing in stocks, or simply trying to improve your personal habits, the wealth mindset can guide you to better decisions, greater success, and lasting fulfillment. It's about taking control, staying focused on your goals, and remaining adaptable in the face of change. The key is to recognize that wealth is a journey, not a destination—and every step you take is an investment in your future self.

As you embark on this journey to financial success, remember that the foundation of your wealth is built from within. Every thought, decision, and action you take is a reflection of your mindset. Mastering your thoughts, beliefs, and attitudes is the first and most important step in your wealth-building journey. Once you master your mind, you will find that the doors to wealth, opportunity, and financial freedom open in ways you never thought possible.

CHAPTER 2: FINANCIAL FREEDOM

Financial Literacy

True financial freedom begins with understanding how money works. It's easy to assume that wealth is something that happens to certain people—those who are born into privilege or who have insider knowledge. But the reality is, financial freedom is not reserved for a select few. It is accessible to anyone who is willing to learn, take control, and make informed decisions about their finances.

The first step toward creating lasting wealth isn't about earning more; it's about understanding the fundamentals of money and how to manage it effectively. This is where financial literacy comes in.

Financial literacy is the ability to understand and make informed decisions about money—whether it's budgeting, saving, investing, or managing debt. It's not just about knowing the numbers, but also about knowing how to make those numbers work in your favor.

Imagine a world where you understand every financial choice you make, from the loans you take to the investments you pursue. That's the power of financial literacy: it gives you control, removes the guesswork, and empowers you to act with confidence and purpose.

Without financial literacy, people are often left at the mercy of the financial systems around them. They might take on high-interest debts without understanding the long-term impact, or they might miss out on investment opportunities simply because they don't know how to assess risk or understand market trends. Worse, many people live paycheck to paycheck because they've never been taught the importance of budgeting or saving. But when you equip yourself with financial knowledge, you stop reacting to life's circumstances and start proactively shaping your financial future.

The first and most critical aspect of financial literacy is budgeting. A budget is more than just a plan for spending—it's a tool for taking control of your finances. It's about understanding how much money is coming in, how much is going out, and making sure that you are putting aside enough for savings and investments.

One of the most common mistakes people make is ignoring their spending habits or thinking that budgeting is restrictive. In truth, budgeting is about freedom. It's about knowing where your money is going and choosing how you want to allocate it in a way that aligns with your financial goals.

When creating a budget, the first step is to track your income and expenses. This gives you a clear picture of where your money is going each month. The next step is to categorize your expenses—distinguishing between needs (rent, utilities, groceries) and wants (luxuries, entertainment, dining out).

By understanding these categories, you can begin to make conscious decisions about where to cut back, where to allocate more, and how to create room for saving and investing. Budgeting also requires discipline and commitment, but it is the most fundamental tool in the journey to financial freedom.

Another important aspect of financial literacy is saving. Too often, people think of saving as something they do after everything else. But in reality, saving should be a top priority, not an afterthought.

The key to building wealth is setting aside money for the future—whether it's for emergencies, retirement, or major life goals. The principle of "pay yourself first" is a cornerstone of financial literacy. Before spending on non-essential items, take a percentage of your income and set it aside.

Over time, these savings will build up, and you'll have the foundation to invest and grow your wealth.

It's important to note that saving and investing are two sides of the same coin. While saving allows you to build up a financial cushion, investing enables that money to grow. Many people make the mistake of leaving their savings in low-interest bank accounts, where it doesn't even keep up with inflation. Financially literate individuals understand the power of investing and seek opportunities to make their money work harder.

Investing isn't just for the wealthy; it's for anyone who understands how it works. There are numerous ways to invest, from traditional stocks and bonds to more unconventional vehicles like real estate, peer-to-peer lending, or starting your own business. The key to successful investing lies in understanding risk and reward. Every investment comes with its own set of risks, but those risks can be mitigated by educating yourself and diversifying your portfolio. Financial literacy involves understanding which investments align with your goals, risk tolerance, and time horizon. The more you learn, the better equipped you are to make smart, informed decisions that will grow your wealth.

Debt is another critical area in financial literacy. Debt is often seen as a necessary evil, but it's something that can easily spiral out of control if not managed properly. There's good debt—such as a mortgage or student loans—that can help you build wealth over time, and then there's bad debt, like credit card debt or payday loans, which only drains your resources.

The key to mastering debt is understanding how to manage it effectively, avoid high-interest loans, and know when it's a good idea to leverage debt for growth.

One of the most important tools in managing debt is understanding interest rates. The difference between a 10% and a 20% interest rate can be the difference between paying off a loan in a few years or being stuck in debt for decades. Financially literate individuals know how to shop around for loans, refinance when necessary, and pay down high-interest debt first. By reducing debt, you free up resources to save, invest, and build wealth.

As your understanding of money deepens, you'll also begin to recognize the importance of long-term planning. Financial literacy isn't just about short-term gains; it's about making decisions today that will pay off years or decades down the road.

One of the most critical aspects of long-term planning is retirement. Many people avoid thinking about retirement because it seems so far off, but the earlier you start saving and investing for retirement, the more time your money has to grow. Understanding how retirement accounts like 401(k)s, IRAs, and other investment vehicles work is essential for building a comfortable retirement.

Finally, financial literacy includes understanding taxes and how they affect your wealth building efforts. Many people overlook the impact taxes have on their income and investments.

Understanding tax laws, tax brackets, and tax-advantaged accounts can help you minimize your tax burden and maximize the amount of money you can invest and save. Financially literate individuals know how to take advantage of tax breaks, deductions, and credits that can significantly improve their bottom line.

Financial literacy is the cornerstone of wealth creation. It's the foundation upon which all other aspects of personal finance are built. The more you understand about budgeting, saving, investing, managing debt, and long-term planning, the better equipped you'll be to create a future of financial freedom. Financial literacy is not a one-time event; it's an ongoing journey that requires continuous learning, adapting, and evolving. As you become more financially literate, you'll begin to see opportunities where others see obstacles, and you'll have the tools to make those opportunities work for you

CHAPTER 3: BUILDING WEALTH THROUGH INCOME

Creating Multiple Streams of Revenue

Wealth doesn't come from one source; it comes from many. For too long, people have relied on a single income stream, typically their job, to build financial security. But as anyone who has achieved true wealth will tell you, relying on one source of income is not only risky but also limiting.

To build lasting wealth, you need to embrace the concept of multiple streams of income. The more sources of revenue you have, the more resilient your financial situation becomes, and the faster you can accelerate your wealth-building efforts.

The idea of having multiple streams of income is rooted in diversification—the practice of spreading your resources across different areas to minimize risk. If you only have one source of income, a job for example, you're exposed to any number of uncertainties. Economic downturns, layoffs, changes in your industry, or personal circumstances can all affect your ability to earn.

However, when you have multiple income streams, you spread out that risk and increase your chances of financial stability and growth.

The first step in creating multiple streams of income is understanding what types of revenue sources are available to you. Income streams generally fall into two categories: active and passive. Active income is money you earn through direct effort, like a salary, wages, or fees for services rendered. It's the time-for-money exchange that most people are familiar with. On the other hand, passive income is money earned with little to no direct involvement, such as through investments, royalties, or businesses that run themselves with minimal oversight.

Both active and passive income are important, but to truly build wealth, the goal should be to balance the two.
Active income can be used to fund investments, grow businesses, or create other passive income streams, while passive income can eventually replace or supplement your active income, freeing up your time and allowing you to pursue other ventures or passions.

One of the simplest ways to start building multiple streams of income is by investing. When you invest, your money works for you, generating returns without you needing to trade time for money.
There are many ways to invest, each with its own level of risk and reward. Stock market investing is one of the most common ways to build wealth through passive income. By

purchasing shares in companies, you become a partial owner and can earn money through dividends and the appreciation of the stock price. But stock investing isn't the only option. Real estate, peer-to-peer lending, and even starting your own business can provide opportunities for passive income.

Real estate, in particular, is a popular choice for those looking to create multiple streams of income. By purchasing rental properties, you can earn regular rental income, and over time, the property's value may increase, offering a significant profit when it's sold. Real estate is a tangible asset that provides income and appreciation, making it one of the most powerful wealth-building tools available. Whether you choose residential, commercial, or vacation rental properties, the key is to find opportunities that fit your financial goals and risk tolerance.

Another source of passive income that has gained popularity in recent years is online businesses. The internet has opened up a wealth of opportunities for entrepreneurs, offering platforms to sell products, offer services, or create content that generates income. Websites like Amazon, Etsy, and Shopify make it easier than ever to start an ecommerce business, while platforms like YouTube, blogging, and podcasting allow individuals to create content that can be monetized through ads, sponsorships, and affiliate marketing. These types of online ventures can generate income on autopilot once they are set up and properly marketed.

Affiliate marketing, for example, allows you to earn commissions by promoting other people's products. This can be done through a blog, YouTube channel, social media, or even email marketing. As you build a following and gain trust, you can recommend products or services to your audience and earn a cut of each sale.

It's a powerful way to earn money without having to create your own products or manage inventory.

Another avenue to create multiple streams of income is by developing intellectual property. Whether it's writing a book, creating a course, or composing music, intellectual property can continue to generate revenue long after the initial creation. Royalties from books, music, patents, or licensing deals can become a significant passive income stream.

The beauty of intellectual property is that once you've created something of value, it can continue to pay you for years to come, often without any additional effort on your part.

For those who prefer active income, starting a side business or freelance work can be an excellent way to build additional revenue streams. Whether you're a skilled writer, graphic designer, web developer, or consultant, there are endless opportunities to leverage your skills and knowledge to earn money on the side. Many people start with freelance work, offering their services on platforms like Fiverr, Upwork, or Freelancer. As your reputation grows, so too does your ability to command higher rates and take on more clients, eventually turning your side hustle into a full-fledged business.

It's important to note that while multiple income streams can provide significant financial benefits, they also require effort and management. It's easy to think that simply having multiple streams will automatically lead to wealth, but in reality, it takes time and strategy to set up and maintain these sources of income.

This is why balancing active and passive income is crucial. Active income, while valuable, can become a burden if it takes up too much of your time. On the other hand, passive income may take a while to build before it becomes substantial. A well-rounded approach, combining the two, will ensure that you can earn money while also creating financial freedom.

A key to building wealth through multiple income streams is reinvestment. As you generate more income, it's essential to reinvest a portion of it into further income-producing assets. The more you invest, the more wealth you can build. This could mean buying more rental properties, investing in more stocks, or scaling your online business. By reinvesting your earnings, you take advantage of compound growth, which accelerates wealth creation over time.

As your portfolio of income streams grows, so does your ability to weather financial storms. If one income stream slows down, others can keep the momentum going. This resilience is one of the key benefits of having multiple streams. It reduces your financial dependence

The earlier you start, the more time your investments have to grow and compound. This is why the concept of "time in the market" is often more important than trying to time the market. The longer you let your investments sit and grow, the greater their potential return.

Before diving into different investment vehicles, it's important to understand that all investments come with some level of risk. There is no such thing as a 100% risk-free investment, but risk can be managed through knowledge, diversification, and strategy. The key is to align your investments with your risk tolerance, financial goals, and time horizon. Some investors may prefer low-risk investments that offer stability, while others may be willing to take on higher risks in exchange for potentially higher returns.

One of the most well-known and accessible investment options is the stock market. When you invest in stocks, you're essentially buying

on any single source, providing both security and flexibility.

In the world of wealth-building, diversification is not just a strategy; it's a mindset. The more you expand your understanding of different income-generating opportunities, the more you can take advantage of the changing financial landscape. Building wealth through multiple streams of revenue is not just about having more money—it's about creating a financial ecosystem where your resources are constantly working for you, allowing you to focus on your passions, explore new ventures, and ultimately, enjoy the freedom that comes with financial independence.

CHAPTER 4: The POWER OF INVESTMENTS

Making Your Money Work for You

Investing is the bridge between earning money and building lasting wealth. While earning through active income is important, it's investing that transforms your financial future. It's the key that unlocks the potential for growth beyond your regular paycheck. The concept is simple: you use your money to generate more money. But the power of investing goes beyond just making money; it's about making your money work tirelessly for you, multiplying itself without you having to constantly trade time for it.

At the core of every successful wealth-building strategy is a solid investment plan. Investment isn't just for the wealthy—it's a tool that anyone can use to build long-term wealth. The sooner you start investing, the more you can take advantage of time and compound interest, which work together to create exponential growth.

In a world where inflation continuously erodes the purchasing power of cash, investing becomes a necessity to preserve and grow your wealth. Without it, your savings may not even keep up with the rising cost of living.

The primary goal of investing is to create income-generating assets that provide you with returns. Whether that's through dividends, interest, capital gains, or rental income, investments allow your money to compound over time, ultimately leading to wealth accumulation.

CHAPTER 4: The POWER OF INVESTMENTS

Making Your Money Work for You

Investing is the bridge between earning money and building lasting wealth. While earning through active income is important, it's investing that transforms your financial future. It's the key that unlocks the potential for growth beyond your regular paycheck. The concept is simple: you use your money to generate more money. But the power of investing goes beyond just making money; it's about making your money work tirelessly for you, multiplying itself without you having to constantly trade time for it.

on any single source, providing both security and flexibility.

In the world of wealth-building, diversification is not just a strategy; it's a mindset. The more you expand your understanding of different income-generating opportunities, the more you can take advantage of the changing financial landscape. Building wealth through multiple streams of revenue is not just about having more money—it's about creating a financial ecosystem where your resources are constantly working for you, allowing you to focus on your passions, explore new ventures, and ultimately, enjoy the freedom that comes with financial independence.

The earlier you start, the more time your investments have to grow and compound. This is why the concept of "time in the market" is often more important than trying to time the market. The longer you let your investments sit and grow, the greater their potential return.

Before diving into different investment vehicles, it's important to understand that all investments come with some level of risk. There is no such thing as a 100% risk-free investment, but risk can be managed through knowledge, diversification, and strategy. The key is to align your investments with your risk tolerance, financial goals, and time horizon. Some investors may prefer low-risk investments that offer stability, while others may be willing to take on higher risks in exchange for potentially higher returns.

One of the most well-known and accessible investment options is the stock market. When you invest in stocks, you're essentially buying

At the core of every successful wealth-building strategy is a solid investment plan. Investment isn't just for the wealthy—it's a tool that anyone can use to build long-term wealth. The sooner you start investing, the more you can take advantage of time and compound interest, which work together to create exponential growth.

In a world where inflation continuously erodes the purchasing power of cash, investing becomes a necessity to preserve and grow your wealth. Without it, your savings may not even keep up with the rising cost of living.

The primary goal of investing is to create income-generating assets that provide you with returns. Whether that's through dividends, interest, capital gains, or rental income, investments allow your money to compound over time, ultimately leading to wealth accumulation.

Another essential part of the investment landscape is bonds. Bonds are essentially loans you make to governments or corporations in exchange for periodic interest payments. While bonds typically offer lower returns than stocks, they also tend to be less volatile and provide a level of stability in a diversified portfolio. Bonds are often used by conservative investors or those looking to balance their portfolios with more predictable income streams.

Real estate is another powerful investment vehicle that has helped countless people create significant wealth. Whether it's through buying rental properties, flipping houses, or investing in commercial real estate, real estate offers multiple ways to generate income. Rental properties, in particular, provide a steady stream of cash flow through tenant payments. Over time, the property's value may also appreciate, allowing you to sell for a profit. Unlike stocks, real estate is a tangible asset that ownership in a company. The value of your shares can rise as the company grows, but it can also fall if the company performs poorly. The stock market can be volatile in the short term, but over the long term, it has historically delivered strong returns. This is why stock investing is considered a cornerstone of wealth-building.

Dividend-paying stocks are one of the most popular ways to generate passive income from investments. When you invest in dividend stocks, you receive regular payouts, often quarterly, based on the company's earnings. This creates a steady stream of income, in addition to the potential for capital appreciation (the increase in stock price over time). Dividend stocks can be especially appealing for those looking to create income without selling their shares. They provide a consistent, reliable source of revenue that can be reinvested to accelerate your wealth-building journey.

can be leveraged (using debt to increase the size of your investment) and offers various tax advantages, making it a favored asset class for many investors.

Real estate investment trusts (REITs) provide an easy way to invest in real estate without having to own and manage physical properties. REITs are companies that own and operate income-producing real estate. When you invest in a REIT, you're buying shares of the company, much like investing in stocks. REITs typically offer high dividend yields and can provide exposure to a diversified portfolio of real estate assets without the hassle of direct property management.

While traditional investments like stocks and real estate are widely known, newer investment vehicles have emerged in recent years that offer exciting opportunities. Cryptocurrencies, for example, have garnered significant attention as both an asset class and a new way to think about value. Cryptocurrencies like Bitcoin, Ethereum, and others have the potential for high returns, but they are also highly volatile and speculative. For investors willing to take on risk, cryptocurrencies can be a way to diversify and explore new frontiers in the financial world. However, it's crucial to understand the technology behind cryptocurrencies and to approach them with caution, as the market can fluctuate dramatically.

Alternative investments such as peer-to-peer lending, precious metals, and commodities are also gaining popularity. Peer-to-peer lending allows you to lend money directly to individuals or businesses in exchange for interest payments. Precious metals, like gold and silver, have long been considered safe-haven assets during times of economic uncertainty, while commodities like oil, agricultural products, and natural resources offer opportunities to invest in real-world assets.

The beauty of investing is that it opens up countless possibilities to create a portfolio that aligns with your goals, time horizon, and risk tolerance. As you build your wealth, the key is to diversify your investments. Diversification means spreading your money across different types of assets—stocks, bonds, real estate, commodities, and more—in order to reduce risk. A well-diversified portfolio ensures that if one asset class underperforms, others may be performing well, thereby smoothing out the ups and downs of the market.

Another important concept in investing is dollar-cost averaging. This strategy involves investing a fixed amount of money at regular intervals, regardless of market conditions. By consistently investing over time, you avoid trying to time the market, which can be a dangerous and often fruitless exercise. Dollar-cost averaging takes advantage of market fluctuations, allowing you to buy more shares when prices are low and fewer shares when prices are high. This strategy can help smooth out the volatility in the market and lower the average cost per share over time.

While it's important to be knowledgeable about the types of investments available, it's equally important to understand your own financial goals and time frame. Long-term investors are generally more focused on building wealth gradually, while those looking for short-term gains may take a more aggressive approach. Understanding your goals will help you choose the right investment strategy and manage the level of risk you're comfortable with.

One thing that sets successful investors apart from others is their ability to stay disciplined. It's easy to get caught up in the noise of market trends and headlines, but successful investors understand the importance of sticking to their strategy and maintaining a long-term perspective. They resist the urge to panic during market downturns and stay focused on their goals. Patience, discipline, and consistency are the hallmarks of successful investing.

The power of investing is that it allows you to create wealth that works for you. Whether you're building a retirement nest egg, funding your children's education, or creating a legacy for future generations, investing is the tool that will help you achieve your financial goals. It's about making your money grow without you having to constantly work for it. The more you learn about investing, the more you'll realize that it's not just about wealth—it's about financial freedom. And the sooner you start, the more you'll benefit from the power of compound growth and the time-tested principle of making your money work for you.

CHAPTER 5: STRATEGIC SAVING

Protecting and Growing Your Wealth

Saving money is often viewed as a basic financial practice, something we do instinctively to prepare for the future. But when it comes to building lasting wealth, saving is far more than just setting aside a portion of your income.

Strategic saving is about making your money work for you by putting it in places where it can grow, protect it from inflation, and ensure that it remains available when you need it most. It's about understanding the difference between hoarding and saving with intention, and using your savings as a stepping stone toward wealth accumulation.

The foundation of strategic saving is recognizing that your money, when left idle, loses its value over time due to inflation. Inflation erodes the purchasing power of cash, meaning that the money you save today will likely buy you less in the future. This is why it's crucial not only to save but to save strategically. Simply placing your money under the mattress or in a low-interest savings account can actually harm your long-term financial growth. To protect your wealth, you need to consider how best to save it in ways that preserve and increase its value.

One of the first principles of strategic saving is building an emergency fund. An emergency fund acts as a financial safety net, providing you with cash for unexpected expenses like medical bills, car repairs, or job loss. It's essential because it helps you avoid dipping into your investments or taking on high-interest debt when life throws a curveball. The general rule of thumb is to have three to six months' worth of living expenses saved in an easily accessible account, such as a high-yield savings account or money market account. The key here is liquidity—you want the money to be readily available in case of an emergency.

However, an emergency fund, while necessary, isn't enough to build wealth. To truly grow your wealth, you need to go beyond emergency savings and think about the long-term. One of the most powerful ways to protect and grow your wealth is by saving and investing in tax-advantaged accounts. These accounts, such as individual retirement accounts (IRAs), 401(k)s, and health savings accounts (HSAs), allow you to save money while benefiting from tax advantages that can significantly increase the amount you can save over time.

A 401(k), for instance, is a retirement account that many employers offer, often with a matching contribution. This means that for every dollar you contribute, your employer may contribute a certain amount as well. This is essentially "free money" and should be taken full advantage of. By contributing to a 401(k), you're not only saving for retirement but also benefiting from compound growth without paying taxes on your contributions until you withdraw them.

Similarly, IRAs offer tax benefits either upfront or in the future. Traditional IRAs allow you to deduct contributions from your taxable income, while Roth IRAs provide tax-free growth and withdrawals in retirement. The key to using these accounts effectively is to start early. The longer you leave your money in these tax-advantaged accounts, the more it can grow, benefiting from the power of compound interest.

One important aspect of strategic saving is understanding how inflation impacts the value of your savings. While a savings account may provide safety and liquidity, it typically offers a very low interest rate—often lower than the inflation rate. This means that your savings are losing purchasing power over time. To combat inflation, you need to think about placing your money in assets that can outpace inflation, such as stocks, bonds, real estate, or even precious metals like gold.

For many people, investing in stocks is the most effective way to protect and grow their wealth in the long term. While stock markets can be volatile in the short term, over time, they tend to provide higher returns than traditional savings accounts or other low-risk investments. The key to successful investing is diversification. By spreading your investments across a range of asset classes—stocks, bonds, real estate, and commodities—you reduce the risk of any one investment tanking and negatively affecting your wealth.

Real estate is another way to protect and grow your wealth. Real estate investments, whether through rental properties or REITs, tend to increase in value over time, even after accounting for inflation. Real estate can also generate a steady stream of income through rent, which provides an additional benefit. The key to real estate investing is to choose properties in locations with high demand and potential for appreciation. Whether you're investing in residential or commercial properties, understanding the market and doing your research is essential for long-term success.

Precious metals like gold and silver also serve as a hedge against inflation and economic uncertainty. These assets are considered safe havens during times of crisis, as they tend to retain their value when other investments falter. While they may not offer the same growth potential as stocks or real estate, they provide a layer of protection in your portfolio, especially during market volatility.

Another crucial aspect of strategic saving is minimizing your expenses. Wealth isn't just about how much you earn; it's also about how much you keep. One of the most effective ways to grow your wealth is to reduce unnecessary expenses and funnel that money into savings and investments. Start by tracking your spending and identifying areas where you can cut back. This might mean cooking at home instead of dining out, canceling unused subscriptions, or finding more affordable alternatives for everyday items.

One powerful strategy for increasing your savings is automating your finances. Set up automatic transfers from your checking account to your savings or investment accounts each month. By automating your savings, you ensure that you're consistently putting money aside, even if you don't feel like it. Over time, this can lead to significant wealth accumulation, especially when combined with the power of compound interest.

But saving and investing is not just about putting money aside and watching it grow; it's also about being mindful of your financial goals. Whether you're saving for retirement, a down payment on a home, or your children's education, it's important to have clear goals that will guide your savings strategy. When you have a specific target in mind, you can create a plan to achieve it, breaking down the steps into manageable chunks. This gives you a sense of direction and keeps you motivated to stay on track.

As your wealth grows, it's also important to protect it. Strategic saving involves not just growing your wealth, but also safeguarding it from potential risks. One way to protect your wealth is through insurance. Health, life, disability, and property insurance can provide peace of mind and help you avoid losing wealth due to unexpected events. Consider working with a financial advisor to make sure your insurance coverage is adequate and aligned with your financial goals.

Estate planning is another essential part of protecting your wealth. Creating a will, establishing trusts, and assigning beneficiaries to your accounts ensures that your wealth is passed on according to your wishes. Without an estate plan, your wealth could be subject to probate, taxes, and delays. By planning ahead, you ensure that your loved ones are taken care of and that your wealth is preserved for future generations.

Strategic saving is more than just putting money aside; it's about making your money work harder, reducing unnecessary risks, and planning for the future. It's about aligning your savings with your long-term goals and using those savings to protect and grow your wealth.

Whether through tax-advantaged accounts, investing in assets that outpace inflation, or reducing expenses, strategic saving lays the foundation for financial independence and lasting wealth.

The sooner you begin, the more time your wealth has to grow. The more disciplined you are in your savings habits, the more you'll accumulate. But above all, it's important to remember that saving is a journey, not a destination. As your wealth grows, so too should your knowledge, your strategies, and your ability to adapt to an ever-changing financial landscape. Saving strategically means more than just accumulating money—it means building a secure financial future for yourself and the ones you love.

CHAPTER 6: WEALTH CREATION THROUGH ENTREPRENEURSHIP

Leveraging Business Opportunities

Entrepreneurship is the most powerful vehicle for creating wealth. It's more than just starting a business; it's about recognizing and seizing opportunities, building something valuable, and leveraging your skills and resources to generate wealth.

Through entrepreneurship, individuals are able to transform their ideas into tangible businesses that not only provide income but also create long-term wealth. The entrepreneurial journey, while challenging, offers some of the greatest financial rewards—rewarding those who are willing to take calculated risks, adapt, and innovate.

The key to wealth creation through entrepreneurship lies in recognizing the potential of a business idea and executing it with determination and strategy. Unlike traditional employment, entrepreneurship allows you to build your own income stream, determine your own future, and achieve financial independence. Starting a business is often seen as a path to greater financial freedom, but it also requires hard work, resilience, and a deep understanding of how businesses operate.

One of the most important aspects of entrepreneurship is identifying opportunities. Wealth doesn't just come from working hard—it comes from spotting gaps in the market, offering solutions to existing problems, and creating products or services that people need or want. This requires a mindset that is always on the lookout for opportunity, whether it's in an existing industry or a completely new niche. Successful entrepreneurs are not afraid to innovate and disrupt traditional business models, always striving to offer something unique that sets them apart from the competition.

When looking to start a business, it's important to think about your skills, passions, and experiences. Successful entrepreneurs often build businesses that align with their interests and expertise. This not only makes the journey more enjoyable but also increases the likelihood of success. When you are genuinely passionate about what you do, your energy and commitment will carry you through the inevitable obstacles that come with entrepreneurship. However, while passion is crucial, it should be paired with market demand.

A successful business is one that provides value to its customers, so it's important to conduct thorough market research to understand your target audience, their needs, and how your product or service can solve their problems.

Once you've identified a viable business idea, the next step is to create a solid business plan. A well-thought-out business plan serves as a blueprint for your business's success. It outlines your vision, goals, and strategies for achieving them. It also details your financial projections, marketing strategies, and operational plans.

A business plan is not just a document you create to seek funding; it's a tool that helps you focus your efforts and measure progress as you move forward. Investors and lenders also require a business plan to assess the viability of your business idea, so it's essential to present a clear, well-researched plan that demonstrates your understanding of the market and your ability to execute.

Funding is another key element of entrepreneurship. Many successful entrepreneurs have started their businesses with limited capital, but they have been able to leverage other people's money—whether through loans, investors, or partnerships—to grow. There are numerous ways to secure funding, each with its own advantages and risks. Bootstrapping, or using your own savings, is a common method for self-funded entrepreneurs who want to maintain full control over their business.

However, for those who need more capital, seeking external funding through angel investors, venture capitalists, or crowdfunding can be viable options. Each funding route has its own criteria, but all require a compelling business idea and a clear plan for success.

While starting a business may require upfront capital, it's the ability to scale that makes entrepreneurship a path to wealth. Scaling your business means increasing its size and profitability without a corresponding increase in costs. It's about building systems and processes that allow you to grow your business efficiently. Whether it's through automation, outsourcing, or expanding your product offerings, scaling is where wealth begins to compound. As your business grows, your potential for generating revenue increases, often at a much faster rate than your operating costs.

One of the most important factors in scaling a business is the ability to delegate and build a team. As an entrepreneur, you may start by doing everything yourself, but as your business grows, you'll need to surround yourself with talented individuals who can contribute their expertise.

A strong team can help you implement your vision and manage the day-to-day operations of your business, allowing you to focus on higher-level strategy and growth. Building a strong company culture and fostering a collaborative environment is also crucial for maintaining productivity and morale as your business expands.

While entrepreneurship offers significant wealth-building potential, it also involves risks. Many new businesses fail within the first few years due to a lack of planning, poor market fit, or insufficient capital. To mitigate these risks, it's important to approach entrepreneurship with a mindset of continuous learning and adaptation.

Successful entrepreneurs are not afraid to fail—they see failure as an opportunity to learn, adapt, and improve. By staying open to feedback, pivoting when necessary, and constantly refining your business model, you increase your chances of success and position your business for long-term growth.

Entrepreneurship isn't just about the money—it's about creating value and building a legacy. Some of the wealthiest entrepreneurs have built businesses that not only made them money but also had a positive impact on society. Consider entrepreneurs like Elon Musk, who transformed multiple industries with companies like Tesla, SpaceX, and SolarCity, or Jeff Bezos, who revolutionized e-commerce with Amazon.

These individuals didn't just seek profit—they sought to solve big problems and change the world, which, in turn, created wealth beyond their imagination.

One of the most powerful aspects of entrepreneurship is the ability to leverage time and resources. While you can't directly control the future, you can control how you allocate your time and resources.

By focusing on activities that will create long-term value, you position yourself to reap the rewards of your efforts down the road. Entrepreneurship is not a get-rich-quick scheme; it's about creating value over time. This long-term mindset is what separates successful entrepreneurs from those who give up too soon.

A critical factor in wealth creation through entrepreneurship is innovation. The most successful businesses are often those that are able to evolve with changing times, technologies, and customer preferences. Entrepreneurs who can innovate and adapt to the market's ever-changing needs are the ones who create lasting businesses that thrive. This requires creativity, a willingness to experiment, and the ability to identify emerging trends before they become mainstream.

As your business grows and matures, wealth creation through entrepreneurship often extends beyond your own lifetime. Building a business that can run independently of you, creating systems that allow it to operate smoothly even in your absence, is a key to true financial freedom. Many entrepreneurs create businesses that are eventually passed down to the next generation, leaving a lasting legacy. Others choose to sell their businesses for a significant profit, cashing in on the value they've created.

Wealth through entrepreneurship isn't limited to those who start massive companies. Even small businesses, when run strategically and efficiently, can generate significant wealth over time. Whether you're starting a service-based business, an e-commerce store, or a brick-and-mortar company, the principles of entrepreneurship remain the same: identify opportunities, build a strong business plan, secure funding, scale efficiently, and innovate to stay relevant. Entrepreneurship is about building something that has value, not only for yourself but also for your customers and the broader community.

While the road to entrepreneurship can be challenging, it's also incredibly rewarding. By embracing the opportunities that come with being your own boss, taking calculated risks, and leveraging the resources at your disposal, you position yourself for wealth creation. Entrepreneurship offers the chance to create lasting financial security, build a legacy, and make a meaningful impact on the world around you. It's about transforming your vision into reality and using the power of business to create wealth, freedom, and success.

CHAPTER 7: THE IMPORTANCE OF WEALTH PROTECTION

Risk Management & Estate Planning

Building wealth is a powerful achievement, but preserving it is an equally critical endeavor. As you accumulate wealth, your financial situation becomes more complex, and with greater wealth comes greater risk. While entrepreneurship, investing, and saving provide the means to accumulate wealth, wealth protection is what ensures that your hard-earned money remains safe and continues to grow. Risk management and estate planning are the two cornerstones of wealth protection, serving as essential safeguards against unforeseen events, legal challenges, or economic downturns. Without these elements in place, all the wealth you've built could be jeopardized.

Risk management is the practice of identifying, assessing, and mitigating the various risks that could threaten your wealth.

Every financial decision you make carries some degree of risk, from investments to business ventures to personal spending. While it's impossible to eliminate risk entirely, you can reduce exposure and make informed choices that protect your assets. By implementing strong risk management strategies, you can safeguard your wealth and ensure that it continues to grow, even in the face of uncertainty.

One of the first steps in risk management is understanding the types of risks that could affect your wealth. There are several key categories to consider:

Market Risk: This is the risk that your investments may lose value due to fluctuations in the market. Stock prices, bond yields, and real estate values can all be affected by economic conditions, political events, or market sentiment. While you can't control the market, you can manage market risk by diversifying your investments. A diversified portfolio spreads your investments across different asset classes (stocks, bonds, real estate, commodities), which helps minimize the impact of any single investment underperforming.

Liquidity Risk: Liquidity risk refers to the difficulty of converting assets into cash without significant loss in value. For example, real estate properties can take time to sell, and some investments, like private equity or collectibles, may be hard to liquidate when needed. To manage liquidity risk, it's important to have a balance of liquid assets—such as cash, bonds, or stocks—that can be quickly converted into money without substantial losses. This ensures you have access to funds in emergencies.

Inflation Risk: Inflation erodes the purchasing power of money, meaning that the money you save today may not have the same value in the future. To mitigate inflation risk, it's crucial to invest in assets that tend to outpace inflation, such as stocks, real estate, or commodities like gold. Over time, these assets generally provide returns that help maintain or grow your wealth, even in the face of rising prices.

Legal and Liability Risk: Your wealth could be at risk if you are sued or involved in a legal dispute. Lawsuits can deplete your assets through legal fees or settlement payments. To protect yourself, consider liability insurance, including umbrella insurance, which provides additional coverage above and beyond your standard insurance policies. For business owners, it's also wise to incorporate your business to limit personal liability and protect your personal assets.

Health and Disability Risk: Unexpected health issues or disabilities can disrupt your ability to work or manage your finances. Health insurance, life insurance, and disability insurance are essential tools to manage these risks. These policies ensure that you are financially protected in the event of illness, injury, or death, allowing you to maintain your lifestyle and protect your wealth for future generations.

To effectively manage these risks, you need a comprehensive approach. This means understanding your risk tolerance—how much risk you're willing to take—and using a mix of strategies, such as diversification, insurance, and contingency planning, to reduce exposure to risk. The more proactive you are in identifying and mitigating risks, the more secure your wealth will be.

Once you've taken steps to manage risk, the next crucial aspect of wealth protection is estate planning. Estate planning is the process of arranging for the transfer of your wealth and assets after your death. Without an estate plan, your assets could be subject to probate, taxes, and legal disputes, potentially leaving your loved ones with little to inherit. Estate planning ensures that your wealth is distributed according to your wishes, minimizing tax burdens and providing for the future of your family.

The core components of estate planning include:

Wills: A will is a legal document that outlines how you want your assets to be distributed after your death. It can designate guardians for minor children, assign beneficiaries to your assets, and specify your funeral wishes. A will is essential for ensuring that your estate is divided according to your desires. Without a valid will, your estate will be distributed according to the state's laws, which may not align with your preferences.

Trusts: A trust is a legal arrangement where a trustee holds and manages assets for the benefit of your beneficiaries. Trusts are often used to avoid probate, reduce estate taxes, and provide for specific needs, such as funding a child's education or supporting a charitable cause. There are various types of trusts, including revocable trusts (which can be altered during your lifetime) and irrevocable trusts (which cannot be changed once established). Trusts provide more flexibility than a will and offer greater privacy, as they do not go through the public probate process.

Power of Attorney: A power of attorney designates someone to manage your financial affairs if you are incapacitated. This document ensures that someone you trust can handle your finances, pay bills, and make investment decisions on your behalf if you are unable to do so. Having a durable power of attorney in place helps protect your wealth in the event of illness or injury.

<u>Healthcare Directives:</u> Healthcare directives, also known as living wills, specify your wishes regarding medical treatment if you become unable to communicate. These documents can outline your preferences for life-saving treatments, organ donation, and end-of-life care. Having a healthcare directive in place gives you control over your medical decisions and ensures your family knows your wishes.

Beneficiary Designations: Certain assets, like life insurance policies, retirement accounts, and bank accounts, allow you to designate beneficiaries who will inherit the assets upon your death. These designations override your will, so it's important to keep them up to date. Review your beneficiary designations periodically to ensure they align with your current wishes and life circumstances.

Estate planning isn't just for the wealthy. Everyone, regardless of net worth, can benefit from having an estate plan in place. It ensures that your assets are protected, your family is cared for, and your wishes are honored. It also helps minimize taxes and probate costs, allowing more of your wealth to be passed down to your loved ones.

One of the most valuable aspects of estate planning is its ability to preserve wealth for future generations. By creating trusts, setting up tax-efficient strategies, and designating beneficiaries, you can ensure that your wealth is passed down intact, avoiding the erosion of your estate through taxes, legal fees, or mismanagement. This is especially important for entrepreneurs, business owners, and individuals with significant assets, as it helps to safeguard your legacy.

Wealth protection is not a one-time event but a lifelong process. It requires ongoing attention and adjustment as your wealth grows, your family's needs change, and laws evolve. To stay ahead, work with a team of professionals—including financial planners, tax advisors, and estate attorneys—who can help you navigate the complexities of risk management and estate planning. These experts can ensure that your strategies are aligned with your long-term financial goals and provide guidance on how to best protect your wealth.

As your wealth continues to grow, so too should your understanding of how to protect it. Wealth protection is not only about safeguarding your assets today but also about securing your future, providing for your loved ones, and leaving a lasting legacy. By combining strategic risk management with thoughtful estate planning, you can ensure that the wealth you've worked hard to build will be preserved, protected, and passed onto future generations.

In the end, wealth protection is about taking a proactive, forward-thinking approach to your financial security. It's about preparing for the unexpected, ensuring that your wealth is shielded from risks, and creating a plan that allows your wealth to thrive for years to come. When you take the time to develop a comprehensive risk management strategy and a robust estate plan, you ensure that your legacy is secure—and that your wealth will continue to grow and benefit those you care about most.

CHAPTER 8: GIVING BACK

Wealth Beyond Money and the Legacy

Wealth is often viewed in terms of money—an accumulation of financial resources, assets, and material goods. But true wealth extends beyond monetary value. It's the impact you have on others, the difference you make in the world, and the legacy you leave behind. The most fulfilling aspect of wealth isn't what it can buy you, but what it enables you to give back to the community, to causes that matter, and to future generations. As you accumulate wealth, it becomes your responsibility—and your privilege—to consider how it can be used for the greater good.

Giving back is a powerful form of wealth. It's a reminder that money, while important, is just one part of the equation. Wealth isn't just about personal gain; it's about using your resources, influence, and time to make a positive impact in the lives of others. This can take many forms—philanthropy, social entrepreneurship, community service, or simply mentoring others. Giving back creates a ripple effect that extends far beyond the immediate recipient. It helps build stronger communities, supports those in need, and fosters a sense of shared purpose that connects individuals across socioeconomic backgrounds.

For many, the desire to give back begins when they reach a certain level of financial success. This may be due to a sense of gratitude, a recognition of privilege, or the realization that money alone doesn't lead to fulfillment. Once the basic needs are met, many individuals seek to use their wealth in ways that will leave a lasting, positive impact. Giving back isn't limited to the wealthy elite; everyone can make a difference, regardless of their financial standing. It's the intention and action that matter most. Whether it's contributing to a charity, funding educational initiatives, or volunteering time, each small act of generosity can have a profound effect.

The concept of wealth as a tool for change is not new. Throughout history, individuals who have amassed significant fortunes have often used their wealth to support social causes and bring about transformative change. Figures like Andrew Carnegie, who funded libraries across the United States, or Bill and Melinda Gates, who established a global health and education foundation, understood that wealth had the potential to solve problems on a large scale. But giving back doesn't require a fortune. The key is to find ways to make a meaningful contribution, however big or small. Your wealth, expertise, and influence can help others in ways that money alone cannot.

One of the most profound ways to give back is through philanthropy. Philanthropy involves giving money, time, or resources to charitable causes, non-profits, or individuals in need. It's an intentional, strategic way to create social change, support communities, and address pressing global issues like poverty, education, healthcare, and environmental sustainability. Whether you choose to fund a specific project, donate to a cause close to your heart, or set up a charitable foundation, philanthropy is a powerful way to channel your wealth into meaningful work.

However, giving back is not just about financial donations. Volunteering your time and expertise can be just as impactful.

Whether you mentor a young entrepreneur, teach financial literacy to underserved communities, or offer professional services pro bono, these contributions help empower others to improve their own lives and achieve their potential. There's a deep sense of fulfillment that comes from using your knowledge and skills to elevate others.

Social entrepreneurship is another growing avenue for those who want to use their business skills for good. Social entrepreneurs create businesses with a dual purpose: to be financially sustainable while also solving social or environmental problems.

By reinvesting profits into their missions, these businesses can create lasting, positive change. Companies like TOMS Shoes, which donates a pair of shoes for every pair sold, or Warby Parker, which provides eyeglasses to those in need, exemplify how entrepreneurship and giving back can coexist.

Wealth can also be used as a means to leave a lasting legacy that impacts future generations. This is where estate planning intersects with philanthropy. Through charitable donations, bequests, and trusts, you can ensure that your wealth continues to benefit causes you care about long after you're gone. Setting up a charitable trust or foundation allows you to continue your philanthropic efforts, ensuring that future generations benefit from your vision and generosity. Not only does this help sustain your legacy, but it can also reduce the tax burden on your estate, creating a win-win scenario for both your beneficiaries and the causes you support.

Beyond financial donations, legacy-building comes from the values and principles you instill in your family, community, and employees.

The lessons you pass down—about integrity, responsibility, and generosity—are just as valuable as the wealth you leave behind.

In fact, the greatest legacy you can leave is one that shapes future generations in meaningful ways. Teaching your children, for example, how to handle wealth responsibly and with empathy can ensure that your wealth is used to benefit others, creating a cycle of giving that extends through the generations.

Wealth also offers the opportunity to address systemic issues and create large-scale change. By supporting policies, initiatives, and movements that promote social equity, environmental sustainability, and human rights, wealthy individuals can influence the direction of society. Philanthropy can support these causes through research grants, advocacy efforts, and policy reform. If you have the resources and influence, you can be a driving force for meaningful societal change, whether on a local, national, or global scale.

But while wealth can certainly make a difference, it's important to remember that it's not the only way to give back. Acts of kindness, empathy, and support are essential components of creating a better world. Wealth can amplify those efforts, but it is not a prerequisite. Even without significant financial resources, individuals can contribute by advocating for those in need, sharing knowledge, and creating opportunities for others.

At its core, giving back is about recognizing that we are all part of a greater whole. When you use your wealth to support others, you contribute to the well-being of the entire community. This sense of interconnectedness is what makes wealth meaningful. True wealth is not what you accumulate but what you contribute. It's the impact you have on others, the lives you touch, and the change you bring to the world. And when you focus on giving back, your wealth takes on a greater significance—becoming a tool for empowerment, healing, and transformation.

The legacy you leave is shaped by your actions and decisions throughout your life. While wealth allows you to create a lasting impact, it is your character, your values, and the kindness you show that will ultimately define your legacy. A legacy of wealth is not just about passing on money—it's about passing on the lessons learned, the values upheld, and the actions taken to make the world a better place.

In the end, wealth beyond money is about creating a life of purpose. The wealth you create through business, investments, or other means is a means to an end—not the end itself. The end is the positive change you bring to others, the lives you touch, and the lasting impact you make. As you accumulate wealth, remember that your most valuable asset is not the sum of your financial resources, but the wealth of goods you do in the world.

When you give back, you ensure that your wealth is more than just a number in a bank account. It becomes a tool for transformation, empowerment, and lasting change. This is the true power of wealth—the ability to make a difference, to leave a legacy, and to create wealth that extends far beyond money.

EPILOGUE

As you reach the end of this book, you've already taken a significant step toward understanding what wealth truly means. But this is not the end—it's only the beginning of your own journey toward financial empowerment, abundance, and legacy. Wealth is not a destination, but a continual process of learning, growing, and making conscious decisions. Whether you are just starting out, or have already accumulated wealth, the principles discussed in these chapters will serve as a roadmap for your future.

The path to wealth is unique for everyone. It's shaped by your individual values, goals, and circumstances. Some will find wealth through entrepreneurship, others through investments, and many through a combination of strategies. However, the core principles remain the same: the mindset that drives you, the financial literacy you acquire, the decisions you make, and most importantly, the impact you leave behind. As you continue to build wealth, remember that it's not just about the money—it's about using that wealth to create a life of purpose, security, and fulfillment.

The true measure of wealth isn't the size of your bank account or the number of assets you hold; it's the legacy you build, the lives you touch, and the positive change you create in the world. Wealth becomes truly powerful when it's used to uplift others, to create opportunities, and to leave a mark that outlasts your lifetime. The generosity, empathy, and integrity you bring into your financial decisions will not only enhance your personal well-being but will ripple out into your community and the world.

As you reflect on the lessons shared here, think about your own personal goals for wealth and how they align with your values. What impact do you want to have? How do you want to be remembered? Your wealth can be a tool for transformation, both in your own life and in the lives of others.

Every decision you make, every action you take, contributes to the broader story of your financial journey. Whether through investments, entrepreneurship, or philanthropy, know that you hold the power to shape the future.

The road to wealth may not always be easy, but it is deeply rewarding. With perseverance, a strong mindset, and the right strategies, you can achieve the financial freedom and security you desire. And as you do, remember that the most meaningful wealth is that which you share—whether it's through giving back, helping others, or creating a lasting legacy.

Your journey to wealth, purpose, and fulfillment is just beginning. Step forward with confidence, knowing that the choices you make today will shape your tomorrow

www.ingramcontent.com/pod-product-compliance
Lightning Source LLC
Chambersburg PA
CBHW071105240526
45469CB00006BD/2341